START-A-CRAFT

Stained Glass

Get started in a new craft with easy-to-follow

projects for beginners

LYNETTE WRIGLEY AND MARC GERSTEIN

CHARTWELL
BOOKS, INC

A QUINTET BOOK

Published by Chartwell Books
A Division of Book Sales, Inc.
110 Enterprise Avenue
Secaucus, New Jersey 07094

ISBN 0-7858-0056-5

This book was designed and produced by
Quintet Publishing Limited
6 Blundell Street
London N7 9BH

Creative Director: Richard Dewing
Designer: James Lawrence
Project Editor: Katie Preston
Editor: Lydia Darbyshire
Photographers: Paul Forrester and
Laura Wickenden

Typeset in Great Britain by
Central Southern Typesetters, Eastbourne
Manufactured in Hong Kong by
Regent Publishing Services Limited
Printed in China

ACKNOWLEDGEMENT

Thank you to Lead and Light, London for
supplying materials and equipment for
photography.

CONTENTS

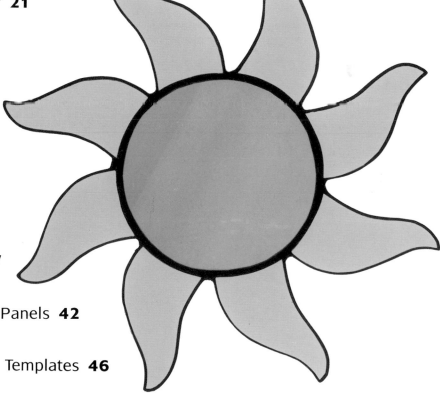

INTRODUCTION

Have you ever looked at something so simple yet so intriguing that you have wanted to try to make it yourself? That is exactly how I became interested in colored glass. Many years ago, I bought a glass lantern in a secondhand store. It was such an attractive and apparently straightforward piece that I decided to try to make one for myself. I eventually found what I thought were the right tools and materials to create a lantern, and I fumbled with the strange tools and experimented with different types of glass until I eventually managed to make something that more or less resembled the object I had wanted to copy. This process was both exciting and extremely frustrating, and the purpose of this book is to provide newcomers to this fascinating hobby with the information that I would have found invaluable in my first efforts in working with colored glass.

Decorative glass work is a large subject, and rather than attempting to cover all aspects of it, this book focuses on the copper foil method, which is the best starting point. The technique of leaded lights, which is usually identified with traditional stained glass windows, is a more complicated and less flexible method. Copper foil, on the other hand, is the method usually associated with the decorative lamps produced by Tiffany & Co. at the turn of the century. It is a versatile method, which can be used to produce window panels, lampshades, and three-dimensional objects that are sturdy, but which look more delicate than similar pieces made with lead.

MATERIALS AND TECHNIQUES

Most crafts have their own vocabularies, tools, and expressions, and when you begin to work with glass you will come across some new terms. In fact, you will need only a limited number of tools to make all the projects in this book, and these will all be readily available from a specialist supplier. If possible, buy from an outlet that works in colored glass, so that you can seek advice from people who are used to working with this material.

BELOW: **A SELECTION OF GLASS TYPES.**

GLASS

Your first visit to a specialist stained-glass store is rather like visiting a restaurant whose menu is written in a language you do not understand. Rolled glass, cathedral glass, new antique — how can you choose which kind you need? In fact, it is a relatively straightforward task, for there are only two main kinds of glass — antique glass and rolled glass.

Antique glass is always handmade — that is, it is mouth-blown. It is the most beautiful glass there is and available in hundreds of colors and tints. It is, however, the most expensive type of colored glass you can buy.

Rolled glass is machine-made, and there are two main kinds — opal glass, which is usually associated with lighting and which is not transparent, and cathedral glass, which is transparent and colored.

Between these two main kinds is a type usually referred to as "new antique," which is simply glass that is similar to antique glass but has been produced by machine. Streaky glass is either antique or cathedral glass in which two colors have been mixed or blended together.

When you select glass for your projects, hold the pieces up to the light to see how different colors work together.

CUTTING GLASS

The most fundamental and important tool you will need is a glass cutter. Basically, it is a pencil-shaped handle with a hardened steel wheel in place of the graphite lead. You can now buy cutters in various shapes and with features such as self-oiling wheels, but they all perform the same task. When the cutter is pushed or pulled across the glass, the wheel scratches or scores the surface. The score will fracture the glass, causing it to break when pressure is exerted underneath the line by tapping.

There are three main types of cutter, and these are distinguished by the type and quality of the cutting wheel.

◊ Steel wheel cutters are the least expensive. However, they are only really sharp for a few days before they begin to lose their edge. They are fine for making a few cuts, but are not really suitable if you want to make progress.

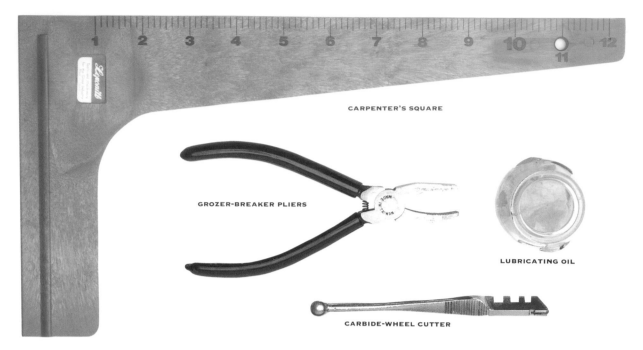

CARPENTER'S SQUARE

GROZER-BREAKER PLIERS

LUBRICATING OIL

CARBIDE-WHEEL CUTTER

◊ Carbide wheel cutters are more expensive than steel wheel cutters, but they are probably the best value. The wheels last longer, and, because they keep their cutting edge, you need to exert less pressure when you are scoring. All the projects in this book were cut with a carbide wheel, ball-end cutter.

◊ Tungsten-end carbide wheel cutters, which are a relatively recent innovation, are available with or without an oil feed. They can usually be identified by their heavier handle, which often contains an oil reservoir. The cutting wheels are smaller than those on steel or carbide cutters, but they are extremely hard and very long-lasting. These are the most expensive type of cutter, but it would be worth buying one if you were going to progress to making more intricate projects.

The conventional pencil-shaped cutter is easy to use, and it has evolved over the years so that it will comfortably fit most people's hands. Buy the best quality cutter that you can afford. Do not be tempted to buy a multihead cutter with several wheels that can be rotated as each one wears out — the head is too large to control when you want to make intricate cuts, and a good quality, single cutter will both last longer and give better results.

USING THE CUTTER

Practice is the single most important factor when you are learning to cut glass. Ask a glass supplier to let you have some small scraps of ⅛ inch clear window glass, which is easy to work with and cheap. Always cut on the smoother side of your piece of glass.

You must lubricate your cutter with light machine oil or mineral spirits so that the

wheel turns freely. Keep a small jar near your working area and keep a cotton ball or something similar soaked in oil in it. Dip your cutter into this every fifth cut or so to keep the wheel turning smoothly. Doing this will also help to prolong the life of your cutter.

Hold the cutter firmly so that you can guide it across the surface of the glass. Use your thumb and index finger to grip the handle, and allow the cutter to make contact with the glass

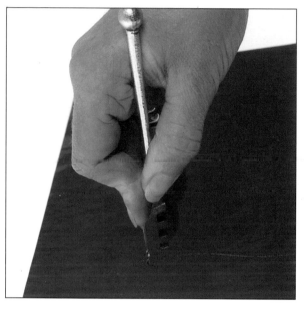

at an angle of 70 or 80 degrees. When you are practicing, begin by placing the cutting wheel at the near edge of the glass and push the cutter away from you to the other edge of the glass, exerting a slow, steady pressure. You will be able to score most types of glass with a pressure of about 10 pounds, and you should almost be able to hear the wheel scoring the surface. Repeat the process again and again. As you practice, you will learn how your cutter works and the best way to hold it. Experiment by adjusting the positions of your finger and thumb slightly and by changing the angle at which you hold the cutter to give a more even line. If your line is too faint, apply more pressure until you can both see and hear the cut line appear.

Remember that you have only one opportunity to score a line — never go over the score twice because this will damage the cutting wheel and will not improve the score.

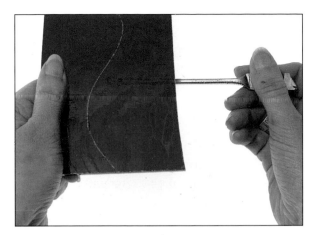

TAPPING

The metal ball at the end of the cutter is used to fracture the score line. Starting from the inside edge, begin to tap directly on the score line from underneath. As you tap, the appearance of the line should begin to change. If it does not, tap a little harder, making sure that you strike the glass directly under the score line. Hold the piece of glass firmly, and remember that gravity will work in your favor and cause the piece to fall onto your work surface.

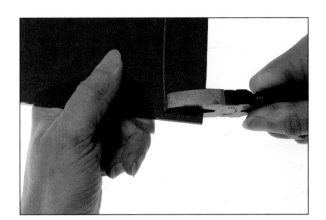

BREAKING

Achieving a clean break is one of the most satisfying aspects of cutting, and you will feel a great sense of achievement when you break along a score line neatly using just your fingers and hands. Hold the scored piece firmly, with a thumb on each side of the score line and your index fingers underneath it. Snap the glass by moving your wrists sharply up and outward.

You can use pliers instead of breaking glass by hand. There are several types of grozing pliers on the market, but one of the most versatile, and the kind that was used for all the projects in this book, is the grozer-breaker combination pliers.

Hold the pliers firmly, place the tip of the pliers as close as possible to the score, and grip the glass. Hold the glass steady in your free hand. Use a sharp downward and outward motion to snap the glass.

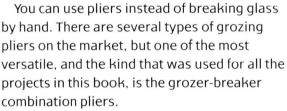

GROZING

You will notice the serrated surface on the inside of the jaws of the grozing pliers. By gripping the glass gently and rolling it backward against the serrated edge, you will be able to remove small sections of glass. Grozing is an important skill when you are shaping glass to match a tracing or cartoon, and you should practice as often as you can on scrap pieces of glass.

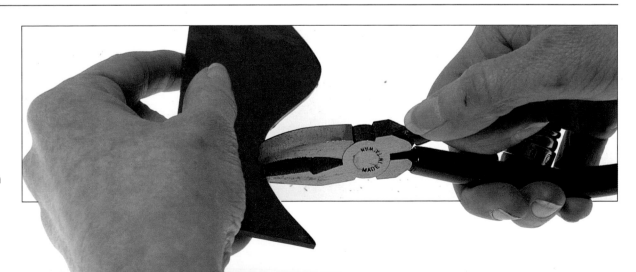

FILING

No matter how well you master the cutting technique, the nature of glass is such that there will always be sharp or jagged edges. A glass file or carborundum stone both smooths off edges, which makes it easier to handle when you apply copper foil, and removes imperfections, giving a better fit. Rubbing down the edge of each cut piece removes tiny burrs and protrusions.

Electric glass grinders are available. These give perfectly smooth edges and are a pleasure to use. Unfortunately, they are rather expensive.

When you have smoothed the edges, always wash all the glass pieces in warm water. This removes any minute particles of glass as well as any traces of oil that have been transferred to the surface of the glass from the cutting wheel. You must make sure that the glass is perfectly clean and dry before you apply copper foil (see below).

SOLDERING

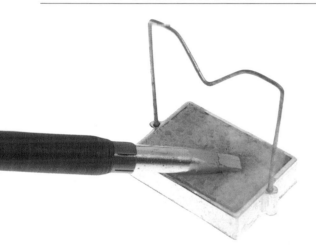

You will need a soldering iron, which melts the solder, thus allowing it to flow along the copper-foiled seams. There are many kinds to choose from, and the choice of additional features makes selection even more complicated than it need be. You will need an iron with a minimum power of 75 watts that is fitted with a plated, screwdriver-shaped tip. The iron coating or plating keeps the tip from corroding. Soldering irons with less power than 75 watts do not give satisfactory results, and you should not use the small irons that are designed to solder electrical connections — these are not at all appropriate for glass work. Keep the head of your soldering iron clean by wiping it on a damp sponge from time to time as you work.

A suitable solder is an alloy of 50 percent tin and 50 percent lead, which will give a clean, neat finish. Solder that has a "core" of flux is not suitable for these projects.

FLUXING

When you use solder, always use a separate flux to allow the melted solder to flow evenly and neatly. A non-toxic flux that gives off a minimum of fumes is ideal. The flux should be brushed onto the joint or seam you are going to solder.

FOILING

Copper foil is used to bond the solder and the pieces of glass together. After each piece has been cut and smoothed and washed and dried, the edges are wrapped with the tape, which should be crimped or smoothed over the surface of the glass to give a stronger finish and a neater appearance. Always begin to apply foil to a section of the glass that is not going to be an outside edge, which will give a neater finish, and overlap the ends of the tape by about ¼ inch.

Copper foil tape is available in a variety of widths, and you should use a width that is appropriate to the thickness of the glass you are using. All the projects in this book were made of glass that is approximately ⅛ inch thick, and the copper foil used was either $7/32$ inch or ¼ inch wide.

CRIMPING

A crimping tool is useful when you press the edges of the foil over onto the surface of a piece of glass. However, you can achieve the same results by bending the foil with your fingers and then pressing it down with a pencil or a thin, pointed plastic tool.

APPLYING SOLDER

There are three distinct soldering processes that you will need to master.

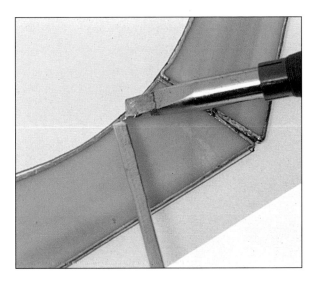

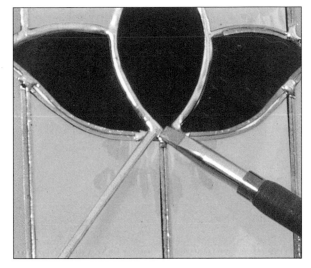

◊ **Tacking** is the method to use when all the pieces are in position and ready for soldering. It is used to prevent the glass from moving while you solder longer seams. Place a dab of flux on the junction of two seams and melt a small amount of solder onto the copper to fuse the pieces of glass together.

◊ **Tinning** is used on edges, on inside pieces, and on the back of panels, etc., that are not seen. Paint the entire seam with flux and lightly coat or "tin" on a thin layer of solder. Use the smallest possible amount of solder, and make sure that you just cover all the exposed copper surfaces.

◊ **Beading** is the technique used on all exterior seams, and it usually requires the most practice. Paint the entire seam with flux and gradually feed solder into the side of the hot iron while you lightly move the iron along the seam. This will create a dome-shaped seam. Clean the iron frequently while you work, wiping the tip with a damp sponge. Try to keep your hand steady and to move along the seam slowly and evenly.

Practice soldering by wrapping two straight-edged pieces of glass in foil. Rub the foil down over the glass, place the edges together, and apply flux to the foiled seams. Use your hot iron to tack solder the top and bottom of the seam. Then touch the seam with the tip of the iron while melting the solder into the side of the tip of the soldering iron. Slowly pull the iron along the seam, moving the iron only as fast as the solder will melt. Re-touch the iron with the soldering stick as and when you require more solder to flow. The iron will not cause the glass to crack if it accidentally touches it.

Whenever you have tack-soldered a point, you must always reapply flux before you can solder the whole seam. Solder resolidifies almost immediately, so that once you have beaded the seams on the front of a piece – the Victorian Panel on page 11, for example – you can turn it immediately to tin the reverse side.

PATINA

Copper sulfate is usually bought in crystal form. The crystals are dissolved in hot water, and the resulting solution is applied to the solder seams with a sponge. The seams will turn a copper-brown color. Black patina is a strong, ready-mixed solution that turns solder seams black; it, too, is applied with a sponge. You must wash all excess patina off the glass. If you allow it to dry, it will stain the glass.

For a high-luster finish, polish all the seams with a metal polish when they are dry and buff them with a clean, soft cloth.

WORK AREA

You will need a sturdy table for cutting and one near an electric outlet for soldering. You will also need to have easy access to running water. You may find it most convenient to have a large board that you can use to protect the tabletop. You will also need a dustpan and soft brush.

SAFETY

Everyone knows that glass is sharp, and because of this people are often reluctant to handle or work with it. However, if you are careful, take sensible precautions, and think about what you are doing, there is no need to worry.

◊ Tiny shards of glass will flake off your cutting lines and should be swept away regularly. Although it may be tempting just to use the side of your hand, don't – this simple action is the cause of most cuts and injuries. Always use a brush to keep your work surface clean.

◊ Keep only the piece of glass you are using on your work surface. Do not allow discarded pieces and scraps to accumulate in a corner. Discard or store them safely.

◊ Handle pieces of glass firmly and confidently. You are more likely to drop something you have not picked up properly.

◊ Always wear suitable goggles or safety glasses when you are cutting or smoothing glass.

◊ A soldering iron gets hot and must be kept on a suitable rest when not in use. If you are not going to use it for a while, unplug it, and if anyone else is likely to be near your work area, let them know that the iron is hot.

◊ Always solder in a well-ventilated room. If possible, have an extractor fan to remove the lead and flux fumes.

◊ The patinas used to tint solder are toxic. Always wear rubber gloves when you apply patina, and keep the unused crystals or solution in a locked cupboard, well away from children.

◊ Always wash your hands carefully after handling lead solder or any chemicals.

If you observe these simple rules, you will find that working with glass is as safe as it is enjoyable.

USING THE TEMPLATES

● For reasons of space all the templates for the projects in this book have been reproduced at half actual size (see pages 46–48). Before you can begin work, you will need to enlarge the outlines and make a few copies.

● The easiest way of enlarging the templates is, of course, by photocopying them. Many libraries, stationery stores, and office equipment outlets have photocopiers with an enlargement facility, and even if the photocopier does not permit you to make a direct enlargement to twice the original size, you can usually enlarge the enlargement to give the necessary dimensions.

● If you do not have access to a photocopier, use the grid method. Using a sharp pencil and a ruler, draw a series of equally spaced lines across and down the original template. If the template has a curved edge, surround it with a rectangle or square so that the edges of the shape just touch the straight edges before drawing the vertical and horizontal lines as before. Take a large, clean piece of paper or cardboard, and draw on it a square or rectangle twice as large as the original. Cover it with vertical and horizontal lines that are spaced at twice the distance of your first grid. For example, if the original is a fairly simple pattern, squares of 1 inch on the original grid and 2 inches on the new grid may be adequate. If the pattern is more complicated, you will probably find it simpler to have a smaller grid – say ½ inch on the original and 1 inch on the enlarged version. Transfer the shapes visible in each small square to the corresponding larger square on the new grid. If necessary, go over the outline with a black felt-tip pen so that it is perfectly clear, even through colored glass.

VICTORIAN PANEL

This pattern is based on the leaded-light door panels that were so popular
in the late 19th century. It is a good introductory project because it requires
both straight edges and some gently curved pieces,
which are slightly more demanding. We have used red, amber, and two
shades of blue, but you can use other colors if you prefer.

You will need

◊ ¼ square foot dark blue antique
◊ ¼ square foot light blue antique
◊ ¼ square foot red antique
◊ ½ square foot amber new antique
◊ ¼-inch copper foil
◊ 10½ ounces solder
◊ Copper wire for loops

Other equipment

◊ Glass cutter
◊ Straightedge
◊ Grozing pliers
◊ Glass file or carborundum stone
◊ Scissors
◊ Crimping tool
◊ Brush (for applying flux)
◊ Soldering iron
◊ Patina

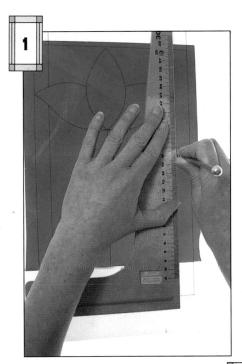

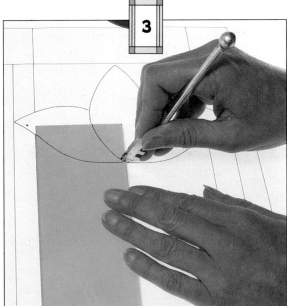

1 Enlarge the template to full size and make two copies. Place the dark blue glass on the pattern and, using a straightedge as a guide, line up the wheel on the inside of the line to be cut. Hold the cutter firmly and score along the line, exerting enough downward pressure on the straightedge to prevent it from slipping while you work. Start from the top edge of the glass and slowly pull the cutter toward you.

2 Place the edge of the grozing pliers next to the score line and hold the glass firmly. Snap off the long pieces using a downward and outward movement of your wrists. Larger pieces can be snapped apart by placing your hands on each side of the score line.

3 All the curves are cut freehand. Start your cut so that you are pressing and pushing the cutter forward over the inside of the cutting line. When you cut a freehand curve, always push the cutter forward so that your hands do not hide the line you are trying to follow.

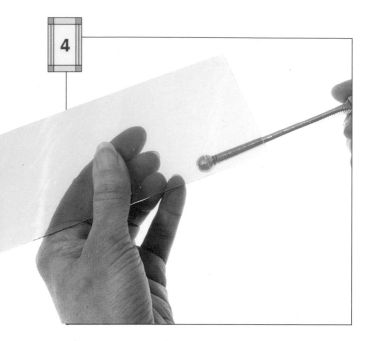

4 Place the ball end of the cutter under the scored glass and begin to tap from one edge to the other. Continue to tap firmly along the score line until the glass is fractured. The piece will now simply break in two; if it does not, you can pull the pieces apart with your hands or with pliers.

5 Continue to cut out all the remaining pieces. Place all the cut shapes on the second template to check for fit, keeping the first copy for cutting, and use grozing pliers to remove any sharp protrusions on the edges. Place the pliers over the section to be removed and exert light pressure, to let the serrated inside surface of the pliers remove the excess glass.

6 Smooth all the pieces with a glass file to remove sharp edges and to make sure that they all fit together well.

TIP

- When you have washed the pieces of glass to remove glass particles and smears of oil, dry them thoroughly.

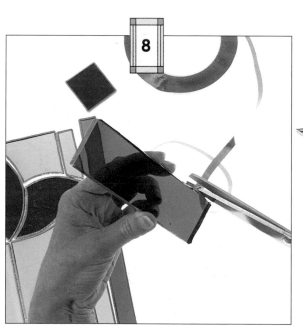

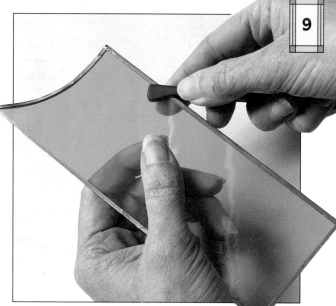

7 Wash all the pieces in water to remove glass dust and any oil that has transferred from the cutting wheel. Dry the pieces thoroughly.

8 Place a strip of foil centrally along the edge of a piece of glass, working all the way around the piece and overlapping the joint by about ¼ inch. Cut off the foil.

9 Use a crimping tool to flatten the foil on both sides of the glass. Apply foil in this way to all the pieces, making sure that it is stuck to the surface of the glass all the way around.

10 Place all the pieces back on the template. Use a brush to apply flux to the areas that are to be tack-soldered.

11 Take the hot soldering iron in one hand and a piece of solder in the other, and melt a small blob of solder at all the points to which you have applied flux. This will help prevent the glass pieces from moving around when you start to run solder down the copper-foiled seams.

FURTHER INFORMATION

Cutting – pages 4–7
Filing – page 8
Foiling – page 8
Fluxing – page 8
Soldering – pages 8–9
Patina – page 10

12 Apply flux with a brush to a whole seam and flow solder along the seam with the hot iron. Feed the solder onto the tip of the iron and work only as fast as the iron will melt the solder. Try to achieve an even, domed soldering line, which is known as "beading."

13 Make loops to hang the panel from either copper or brass. Place the loops on the seam between the red and the blue pieces. Flux and solder the loops in place. Use your grozing pliers to hold the loops because the wire will heat up very quickly and become far too hot for you to hold with your fingers. You must make sure that the loops are attached to a seam rather than simply to the outside edge of a piece of glass. Now continue to tin-solder the back seams and sides of the panel, remembering to add flux before soldering.

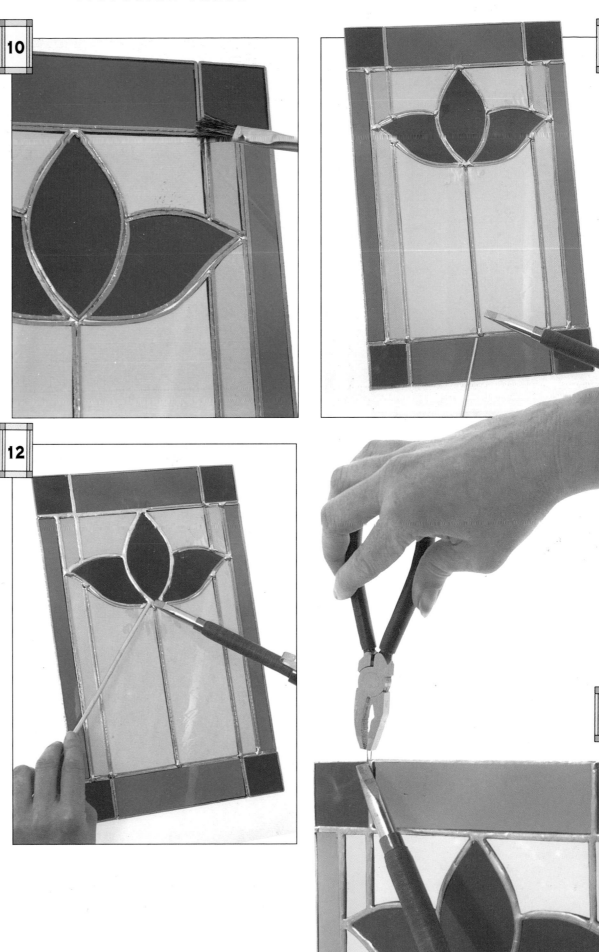

14 Wash any remaining flux off with warm, soapy water.

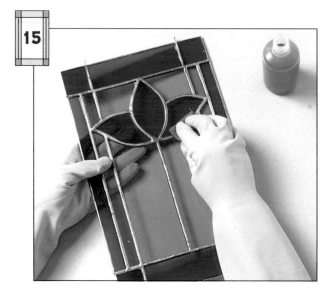

15 Apply the patina with a sponge, but do not dry it. Then wash the whole panel with a soft, nonabrasive sponge and allow to dry. You must be careful to remove all traces of patina from the glass; otherwise, it will stain the surface.

TIP

● When the panel is dry, rub the soldered seams with metal polish to give a bright, even luster.

Sun Mobile

This bright sun involves cutting out only two different shapes, but it does require you to cut out a complete circle. It is an excellent project for practicing your freehand cutting and grozing skills.

You will need
◊ ½ square foot amber new antique
◊ ½ square foot yellow antique
◊ ¼-inch copper foil
◊ 8 ounces solder
◊ Copper wire for loops

Other equipment
◊ Glass cutter
◊ Grozing pliers
◊ Glass file or carborundum stone
◊ Scissors
◊ Crimping tool
◊ Brush (for applying flux)
◊ Soldering iron
◊ Patina

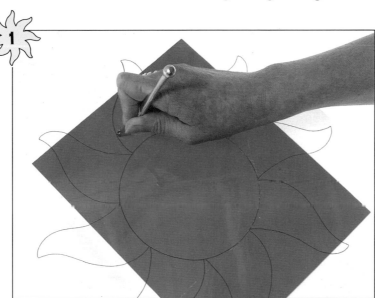

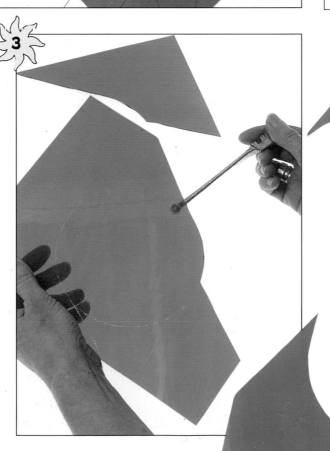

1 Enlarge and make two copies of the template. Transfer your cut pieces to the second copy. Lay the amber glass over the circle and begin to guide the cutter around the outline, pushing and pressing the cutter while you follow the line. When you have gone about a quarter of the way around, run the cutter off the nearest edge in a straight line. Continue to make cuts until you have scored the whole circle.

2 Use the ball end of the cutter to begin tapping under the scored tangential lines and around the scored circle. The extra cuts make the breaking-out process much easier because they relieve the stress on the glass.

3 As you tap the score line, you will find that the excess glass will begin to come away from the circle.

4 Use grozing pliers to break off the jagged edges around the circle.

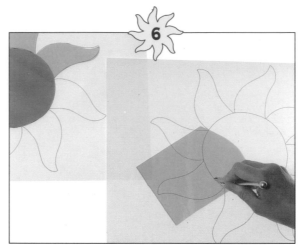

5 Use your pliers to nibble off the rough edges until the edge of the circle is as smooth and even as you can make it.

6 Place a piece of yellow glass over the sun-ray template and begin by cutting the inside curve freehand. Use the ball end of your cutter to tap directly under the score, and if necessary use your pliers to break off the pieces. Cut out eight yellow sun-rays.

7 Use a glass file or carborundum stone to smooth the edges of all the pieces, then wash them in warm water to remove glass dust and any oil that has transferred from the cutting wheel. Dry the pieces thoroughly.

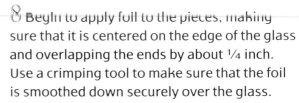

8 Begin to apply foil to the pieces, making sure that it is centered on the edge of the glass and overlapping the ends by about ¼ inch. Use a crimping tool to make sure that the foil is smoothed down securely over the glass.

9 Position all the foiled pieces on the pattern to check for fit, then apply flux to the points at which the rays meet the circle. Tack-solder them together.

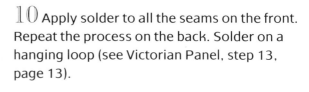

TIP

● Always begin applying foil to a section of glass that is not going to be an outside edge. This will give a neater finish.

10 Apply solder to all the seams on the front. Repeat the process on the back. Solder on a hanging loop (see Victorian Panel, step 13, page 13).

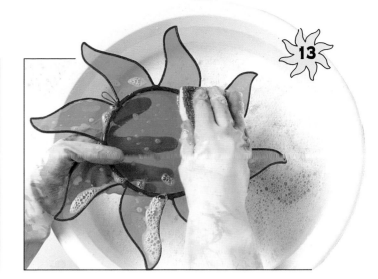

11 Wash the whole piece in warm, soapy water.

12 Apply patina with a sponge.

13 Carefully wash off any excess patina from the glass so that it does not stain it.

FURTHER INFORMATION

Cutting — pages 4—7
Filing — page 8
Foiling — page 8
Fluxing — page 8
Soldering — pages 8—9
Patina — page 10

POTPOURRI HOLDER

This attractive container can be filled with colorful potpourri or sparkling glass marbles. We have used a mixture of clear and pink glass, but you can choose other colors. The project involves cutting out an almost complete circle and will be further practice for your freehand cutting skills.

You will need
◊ 1 square foot clear new antique
◊ ¼ square foot pink antique
◊ ¼-inch copper foil
◊ 4 ounces solder

Other equipment
◊ Glass cutter
◊ Grozing pliers
◊ Straightedge
◊ Glass file or carborundum stone
◊ Scissors
◊ Crimping tool
◊ Brush (for applying flux)
◊ Soldering iron

FURTHER INFORMATION

Cutting – pages 4–7
Filing – page 8
Foiling – page 8
Fluxing – pages 8–9
Soldering – page 10

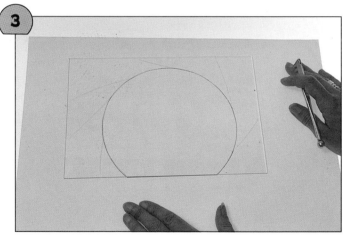

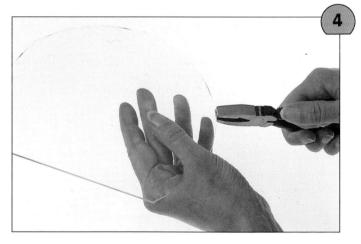

1 Enlarge and make two copies of the template. Place the clear glass so that one straight edge is along the bottom edge of the template and, beginning at a bottom corner, make the first of four cuts.

2 Follow the curve around until it begins to curve sharply, then take the cutter upward in a straight line to the top of the glass. Return your cutter to the curved score line and continue the process.

3 These extra tangential cuts relieve the stress on the glass when you tap the score line, and make it easier to separate the pieces. When you have scored right around the outline, tap gently under the line to separate the pieces.

4 Use the serrated edge inside the grozing pliers to remove all the rough edges. Repeat the process to make a second shape.

5

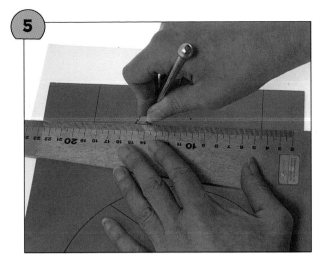

6

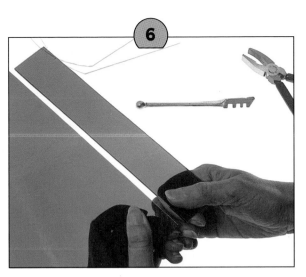

7

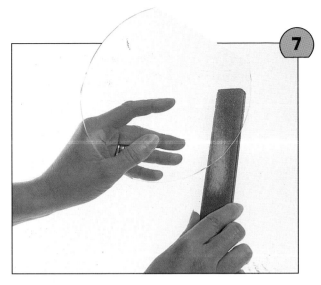

5 Use a straightedge to cut out two pink glass rectangles. Start the score line at the top edge of the glass and pull your cutter toward you, moving it slowly and steadily.

6 Place your fingers and thumbs on each side of the scored line and make a quick movement with your wrists to snap the glass cleanly.

7 Smooth off all the sharp edges with a glass file or carborundum stone. Wash all the pieces in warm water to remove glass dust and any oil that has transferred from the cutting wheel. Dry the pieces thoroughly.

8 Begin to place foil around each piece, taking care to center it. Apply foil all the way around the clear glass pieces, overlapping the ends by about 1/4 inch, but you need apply tape only to the short ends of the pink pieces.

9 Use a crimping tool or pencil to press the foil down firmly over the surface of the glass.

10 Use a brush to apply flux over all the copper-foiled edges, and lightly coat or "tin" on a thin layer of solder. Use the smallest possible amount of solder and make sure that you just cover all the exposed copper surfaces.

8

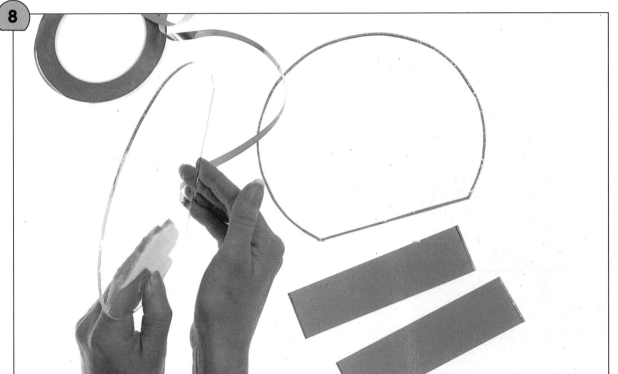

9

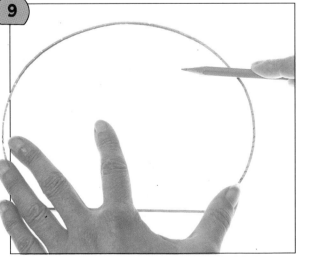

10

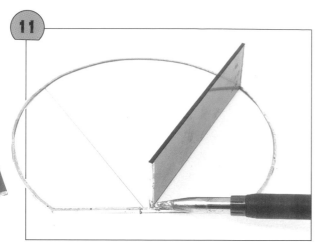

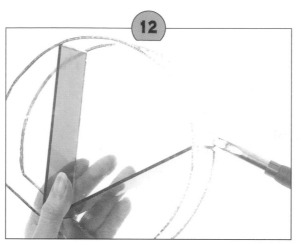

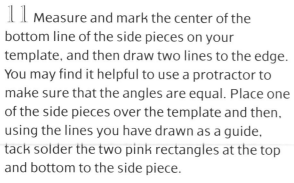

11 Measure and mark the center of the bottom line of the side pieces on your template, and then draw two lines to the edge. You may find it helpful to use a protractor to make sure that the angles are equal. Place one of the side pieces over the template and then, using the lines you have drawn as a guide, tack solder the two pink rectangles at the top and bottom to the side piece.

12 Place the second side on top, making sure that it is positioned accurately over the first, and tack-solder the remaining corners.

13 Carefully wash in warm, soapy water. This piece does not need any patina.

CANDLE HOLDER

This useful article could be used to hold a nightlight candle. It is the first project in this book that involves the use of mirror glass, which should always be cut with the reflective side facing up.

You will need
◊ ¼ square foot of ¹/₁₀-inch mirror glass
◊ ¼ square foot amber new antique
◊ ⅛ square foot green new antique
◊ ¼-inch copper foil
◊ 4 ounces solder

Other equipment
◊ Scissors
◊ Felt-tip pen
◊ Straightedge
◊ Glass cutter
◊ Grozing pliers
◊ Glass file or carborundum stone
◊ Crimping tool
◊ Brush (for applying flux)
◊ Soldering iron

TIP

● Remember to lubricate the cutter from time to time as you work so that the wheel always turns smoothly and freely.

1 Enlarge and make three copies of the templates. Cut out the full-sized mirror piece from one copy.

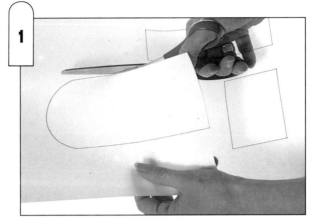

2 Use a felt-tip pen to trace the outline of the template onto the mirror glass.

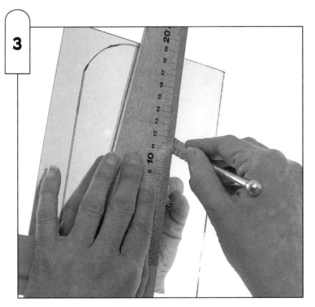

3 With the straightedge along the pen line, use the cutter to score along the straight lines, pulling the cutter toward you with a steady, even pressure. Hold the straightedge down firmly so that it does not slip.

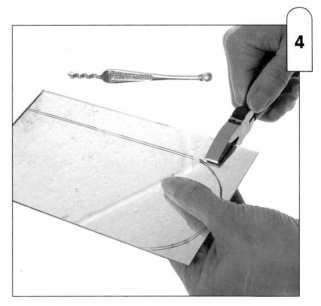

4 Break off the straight cut by placing the tip of your grozing pliers against the scored line and snapping it off with a sharp downward movement.

5

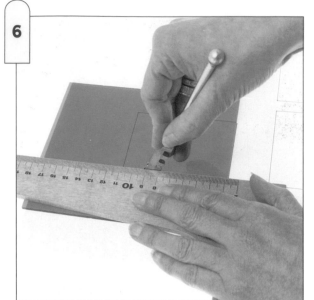

6

7

5 Score the top curve freehand, starting at one edge and pushing the cutter along the felt-tip pen line.

6 Use the straightedge to score and cut out the pieces for the three sides and bottom of the box. Use your grozing pliers to remove any sharp edges, then smooth off all the sharp edges with a glass file or carborundum stone. Wash all the pieces in warm water to remove glass dust and oil, and dry them thoroughly.

7 Begin placing foil around each piece, taking care to center it on the edge and to overlap the ends by about ¼ inch. Use a crimping tool or pencil to press the foil down firmly over the surface of the glass.

8 Use a brush to apply flux over all the copper-foiled edges, and lightly coat or "tin" on a thin layer of solder on both back and front.

9 Assemble the holder by carefully placing the side panel on the side edge of the bottom section. Carefully melt a small amount of solder to hold it in position.

10 Attach the other side panel in exactly the same way.

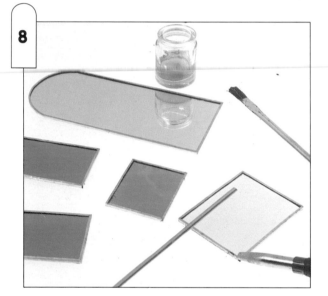

8

9

FURTHER INFORMATION

Cutting – pages 4–7
Filing – page 8
Foiling – page 8
Fluxing – page 8
Soldering – pages 8–9

10

11 Complete the box by placing the front section in position. Tack-solder the seams.

12 Place the mirror in the open side of the box and tack-solder the seams. Solder all the seams where the mirror meets the box.

13 Wash the candle holder in warm, soapy water; use window cleaner to remove any water marks from the mirror.

MIRROR

The mirror project involves making a frame of colored glass, to which the mirror glass is attached, while the green leaf motif is overlaid on the frame.

You will need
◊ ½ square foot amber opal
◊ ⅛ square foot green opal
◊ ½ square foot of $\frac{1}{10}$-inch mirror glass
◊ ¼-inch copper foil
◊ 8 ounces solder
◊ 6–8 inches picture hanging wire

Other equipment
◊ Scissors
◊ Felt-tip pen
◊ Straightedge
◊ Glass cutter
◊ Grozing pliers
◊ Glass file or carborundum stone
◊ Crimping tool
◊ Brush (for applying flux)
◊ Soldering iron
◊ Patina

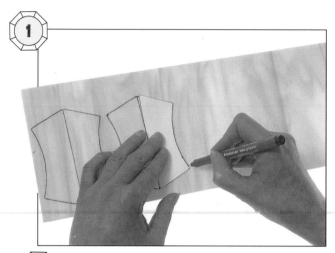

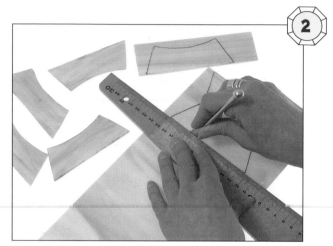

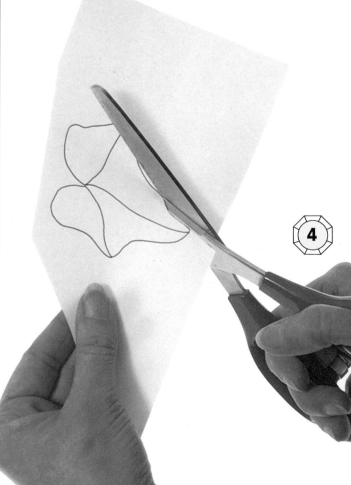

1 Enlarge and make three copies of the template. Cut out all the pattern pieces from one copy. Use a felt-tip pen to mark the border pieces on the glass, laying them back to back.

2 Score the straight line between two border pieces, applying firm, even pressure. Separate the pieces by using a quick snapping movement of your wrists. Turn the short ends in the same way.

3 Score the curved sections freehand. Position the grozing pliers next to the score line and break off the pieces. Repeat for all eight edge pieces.

4 Cut out the pattern pieces for the leaf motif and draw around them to transfer the outlines to the green glass.

FURTHER INFORMATION
Cutting – pages 4–7
Filing – page 8
Foiling – page 8
Fluxing – page 8
Soldering – pages 8–9
Patina – page 10

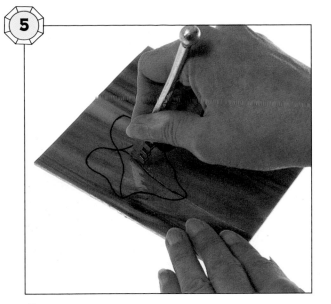

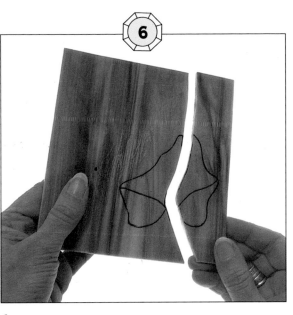

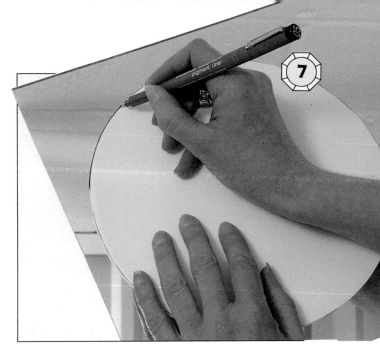

5 Score the glass, starting from the bottom edge and pushing the cutter up through the center of the leaf.

6 Tap the underside of the score line with the ball end of the cutter and separate the pieces. Continue to score and tap out the rest of the motif.

7 Cut the circular template for the mirror and draw around it with a felt-tip pen. The diameter of the mirror needs to overlap the frame by about 1/2 inch all around. Remember that mirror glass always has to be cut with the reflective side up. Score the circle in the same way you scored and cut out the circle in the Sun Mobile, steps 1–5 (page 15).

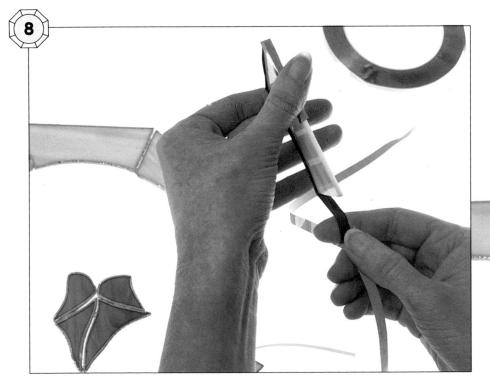

9 Bend the edges of the copper foil over and use a crimping tool or pencil to smooth down the tape.

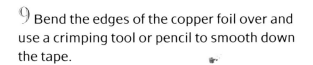

8 Remove all protuberances with your grozing pliers and smooth all the edges with a glass file or carborundum stone. Wash all the pieces to remove any particles of glass and smears of oil, and dry them thoroughly. Wrap all the pieces in copper foil, taking care to place the edge of each piece of glass in the center of the copper tape.

25 =

10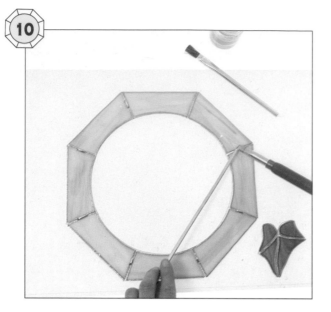

11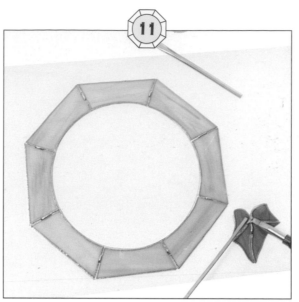

12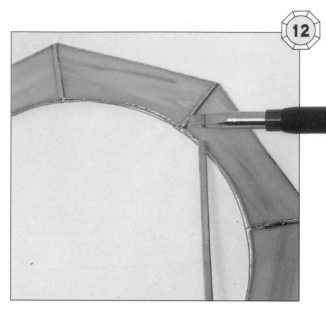

10 Place all the pieces on the template and use a brush to apply dabs of flux to the joints. Tack-solder the pieces together by melting small amounts of solder on the places you have painted with flux.

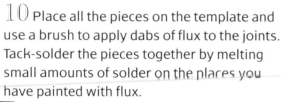

11 Flux and tack-solder the leaf pieces together.

12 Apply flux to all the seams and solder them, using enough solder to form a "bead" along all the seams on the top surface. Apply a fine layer of flux all around the circular hole in the frame and lightly coat or "tin" on a thin layer of solder, using the smallest possible amount of solder and making sure that you just cover all the exposed copper tape. Turn over the frame and "tin" the back joints in the same way.

13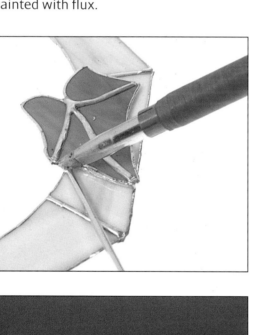

15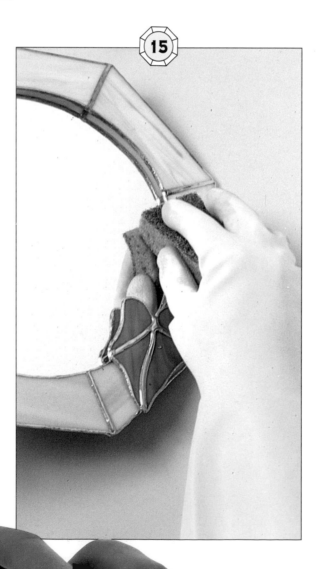

13 Finish soldering the leaf, then attach it to the frame with two spots of melted solder.

14 Turn over the frame and place the mirror on the back, soldering the points at which the frame and mirror meet. Solder a length of picture wire to appropriate joints between the frame and mirror, adding extra solder to make sure that the wire is securely attached.

15 Wash the completed mirror in warm, soapy water, and apply patina to all the soldered joints. Wash thoroughly in warm, soapy water to remove excess patina. When it is dry, clean the mirror with glass cleaner to remove any water marks.

14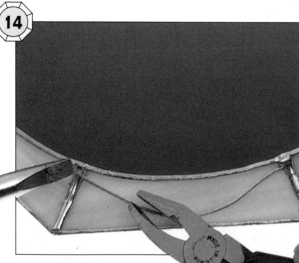

WHALE PANEL

This colorful panel uses the whole range of straight cuts and both inside and outside curved cuts. It is a slightly more advanced project and requires greater cutting skills, so you should practice cutting curves on some scraps of window glass before you start.

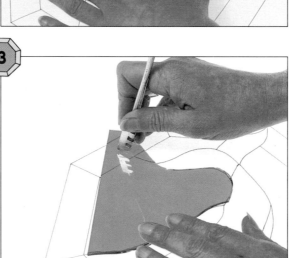

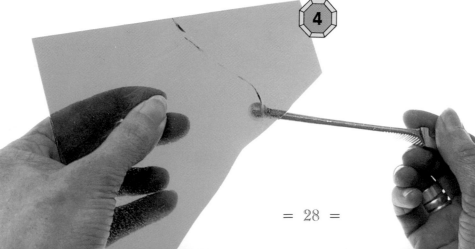

You will need
◊ ¼ square foot dark blue antique
◊ ¼ square foot sea green antique
◊ ¼ square foot mid blue antique
◊ ¼ square foot olive green antique
◊ ⅛ square foot white cathedral
◊ 10½ ounces solder
◊ ⁷⁄₃₂-inch copper foil
◊ Copper wire for loops

Other equipment
◊ Glass cutter
◊ Straightedge
◊ Grozing pliers
◊ Glass file or carborundum stone
◊ Scissors
◊ Crimping tool
◊ Brush (for applying flux)
◊ Soldering iron
◊ Patina

1 Enlarge and make two copies of the template. Lay the dark blue glass over the template and begin to cut out the whale's body. The first scored line should run from the nose – because you should always start to cut from the edge of the glass – along the back and off the side. Press the cutter down firmly while you push, following the template line. Tap the scored line from underneath to loosen the cut and if it does not separate of its own accord, pull with your pliers.

2 Line up the cut edge with the template and make a second score in the same way. Tap from underneath to separate the pieces. Cut out all the dark blue pieces in the same way.

3 Lay the sea green glass over the template. Do not try to cut this tight curve in a single movement. Follow the curved line until it moves sharply to the left, then move your cutter straight to the edge of the glass. Return the cutter to the line and continue, making several tangential cuts as you work around the curve. The tighter the curve you are cutting, the more tangential cuts you should make.

4 When you have completed the line, tap from underneath to loosen the score so that you can break off the pieces.

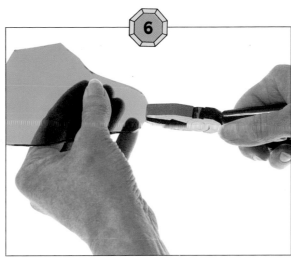

5 If necessary, hold the glass firmly in one hand and use your pliers to pull away the excess glass. Continue to cut out all the pieces in the appropriate colors, remembering to make as many tangential cuts as necessary when you are cutting tight curves.

6 Use your grozing pliers to remove any protuberances.

7 Smooth all edges with a glass file or carborundum stone.

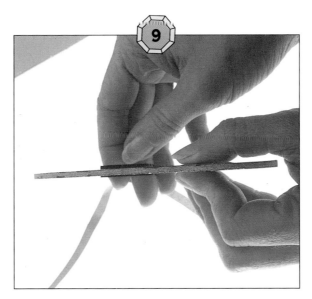

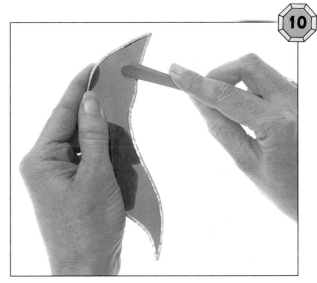

8 Wash all the pieces in warm water to remove glass dust and traces of oil. Dry all the pieces thoroughly.

9 Apply copper foil to all the edges, taking care to center the edge of each piece on the foil, overlapping the ends by about ¼ inch.

10 Flatten and smooth all the edges with a crimper or pencil so that you have a smooth soldering line.

FURTHER INFORMATION
Cutting — pages 4—7
Filing — page 8
Foiling — page 8
Fluxing — page 8
Soldering — pages 8—9
Patina — page 10

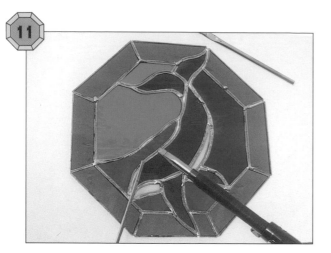

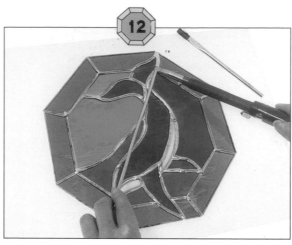

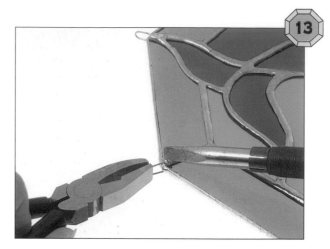

11 Lay the pieces on the template. You will need to tack-solder the pieces so that they do not move when you solder the seams. Use a brush to dab a small amount of flux at all the junctions and melt a small amount of solder onto these points.

12 Flux all the seams and begin to apply solder. Feed and solder into the hot iron while you move the iron slowly and smoothly along the seam. Use enough solder to build up a "bead" on the seam.

13 Turn the panel over and flat-solder the back and sides – do not use so much solder that it forms a "bead." Make and solder on two loops, making sure they are attached to the seam and not just to the outside edge of the panel (see Victorian Panel, step 13, page 13).

14 Wash the panel in warm, soapy water. Apply the patina, taking care to wash the panel to remove all patina from the glass when you have finished.

PLANTER

This large three-dimensional project is more complicated to assemble. While you are working, keep checking the layout and position of the pieces against the template, and use a carpenter's square to make sure that the angles stay at 90 degrees. Remember, too, that opal glass is not transparent, and you will need to make templates to draw around.

You will need
◊ 3 ½ square feet of ¹⁄₁₀-inch window glass
◊ ½ square foot medium green opal
◊ ¼-inch copper foil
◊ 12 ounces solder

Other equipment
◊ Straightedge
◊ Scissors
◊ Felt-tip pen
◊ Glass cutter
◊ Grozing pliers
◊ Glass file or carborundum stone
◊ Crimping tool
◊ Brush (for applying flux)
◊ Soldering iron
◊ Carpenter's square
◊ Patina

FURTHER INFORMATION

Cutting – pages 4–7
Filing – page 8
Foiling – page 8
Fluxing – page 8
Soldering – pages 8–9
Patina – page 10

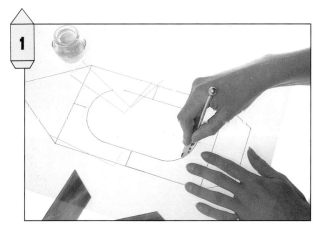

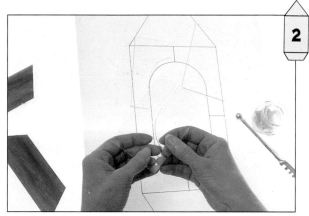

1 Enlarge and make three copies of the template; cut out templates for the sections made from opal glass. Cut out the top sections from clear glass by placing the glass over the pattern and using a straightedge to score the line. Use your pliers to break off the pieces. Trace around the templates for the bottom sections on opal glass before scoring around them as before.

2 Cut 16 rectangular blanks for the sides, and begin to cut the inside curves freehand. Tap the underside of the score line and begin to break out the shape, using your fingers and pliers. Be prepared to make extra pieces for this project, as this is a difficult shape to cut out.

3 When you have cut all the pieces, use your pliers to remove any protuberances, then smooth all edges with a glass file or carborundum stone. Wash the pieces to remove all glass particles and traces of grease. Dry all the pieces thoroughly.

4 Apply copper foil to the edge of all pieces, using the crimping tool to bend the edges over.

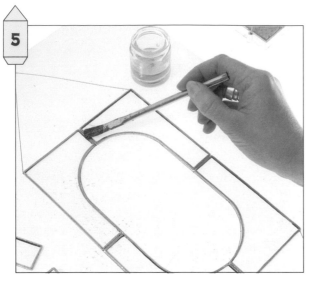

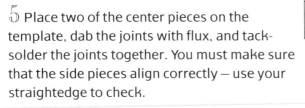

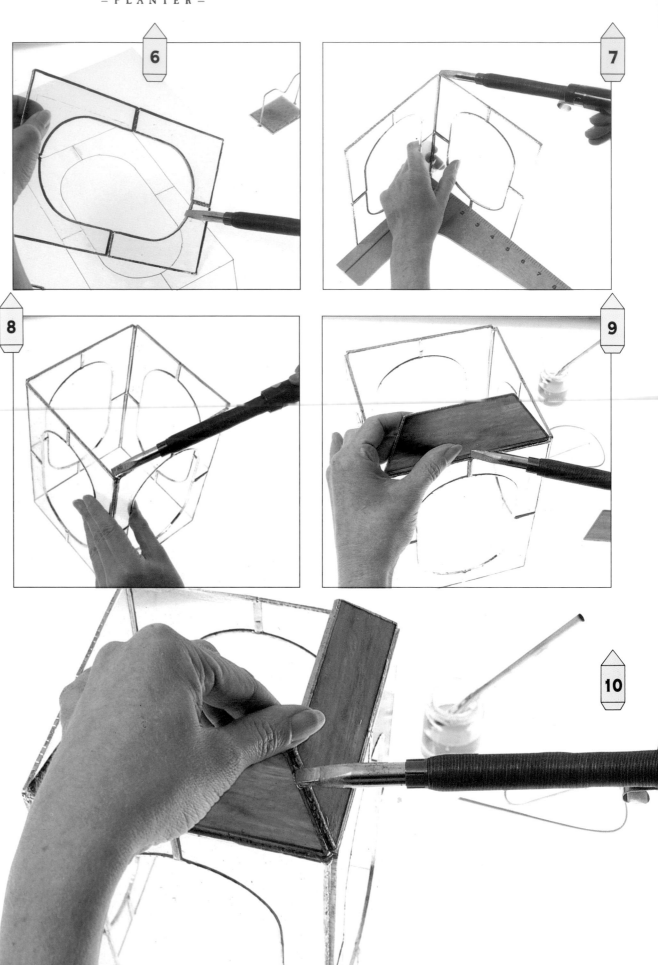

5 Place two of the center pieces on the template, dab the joints with flux, and tack-solder the joints together. You must make sure that the side pieces align correctly — use your straightedge to check.

6 Paint the four seams with flux and lightly coat or "tin" on a thin layer of solder, using the smallest possible amount of solder, just covering all the exposed copper surfaces.

7 Use a carpenter's square or draw a right angle on a piece of cardboard and use it to position two center sections. Place the sections corner to corner and tack-solder the top. Remove the carpenter's square and tack-solder the inside of the bottom edge.

8 Repeat the previous step with the remaining two sections and tack-solder the paired sections together.

9 Position and tack-solder the first opal bottom piece.

10 Continue to tack-solder the second, third, and fourth opal pieces into place, making sure that each is correctly positioned.

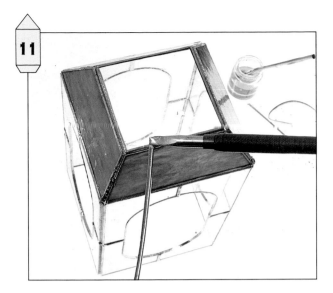

11 Position the clear glass base on the opal section and tack-solder it in place.

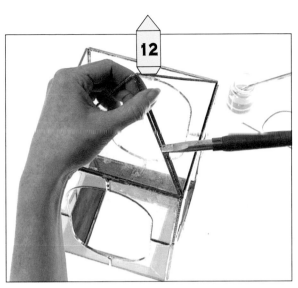

12 Carefully raise the planter so that it is sitting upright on the base. Begin to tack-solder the remaining four top pieces, using the same method as in steps 9 and 10.

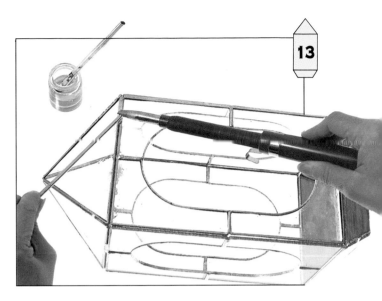

13 Begin to solder the seams. Flux a seam, then feed solder into the hot iron. You will find it easier to solder the side seams if you turn the planter sideways.

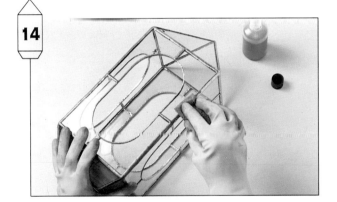

14 Wash in warm, soapy water and apply patina with a sponge.

15 Wash off the excess patina from the surface of the glass.

FISH PANEL

We have deliberately chosen bright colors for this panel, although they are not necessarily the ones you would choose for yourself. When you buy the glass, hold the different colors up to the light to see how they work next to each other. Glass nuggets, which are available from specialist glass suppliers, can be used for decorative details in many projects.

You will need
◊ ½ square foot orange streaky cathedral
◊ ¼ square foot green-brown streaky cathedral
◊ ⅛ square foot dark green new antique
◊ ½ square foot aqua green antique
◊ Glass nugget for fish's eye
◊ 1 pound solder
◊ ¼-inch copper foil
◊ Copper wire for loops

Other equipment
◊ Glass cutter
◊ Straightedge
◊ Grozing pliers
◊ Glass file or carborundum stone
◊ Scissors
◊ Crimping tool
◊ Brush (for applying flux)
◊ Soldering iron
◊ Patina

TIP

● If a score line will not break, keep on tapping it — if in doubt, tap it out.

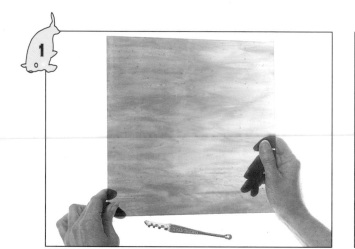

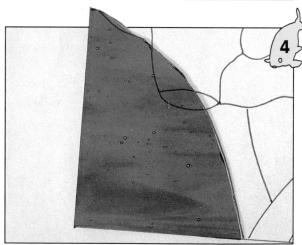

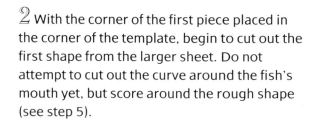

1 Enlarge and make two copies of the template. Look carefully at your pieces of glass before you decide how you are going to place them on the template. Most glass looks better in one direction than another, and you should take this into account when you position the pieces.

2 With the corner of the first piece placed in the corner of the template, begin to cut out the first shape from the larger sheet. Do not attempt to cut out the curve around the fish's mouth yet, but score around the rough shape (see step 5).

3 Tap underneath the score line from one end to the other. The score line should fracture well enough for the piece to break away from the sheet.

4 The piece is now ready for you to score the curve around the mouth. Place it back on the template.

5 Press and push the cutter forward to follow the line of the mouth. Make some extra scores about ⅛ inch away from the primary line. These extra scores will enable you to nibble away the glass with your grozing pliers.

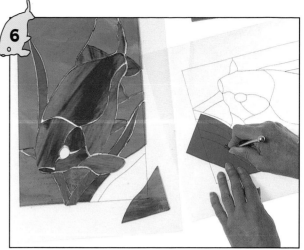

6 Use the same method wherever there are sharp curves — cut out the overall shape and then return to the score to break out the curve. Score all the other shapes and cut out all the pieces.

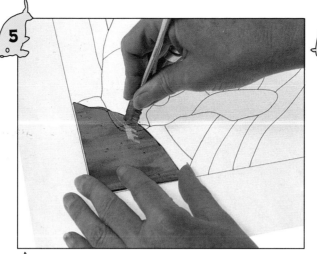

7 Remove any unwanted protuberances with your grozing pliers. Smooth all edges with a glass file or carborundum stone. Wash the pieces to remove glass particles and any traces of grease and dry them thoroughly. Apply copper foil around all the pieces, making sure it is centered on the glass and overlapping the ends by about ¼ inch.

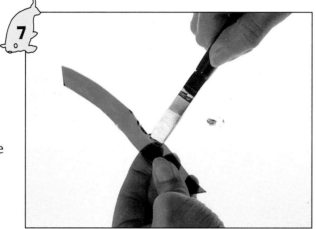

8 File the glass nugget before adding foil. Use a crimping tool to press the foil down around all the pieces.

9 Place the pieces on the template, and flux and tack-solder them together so that they do not move out of position when you solder the seams.

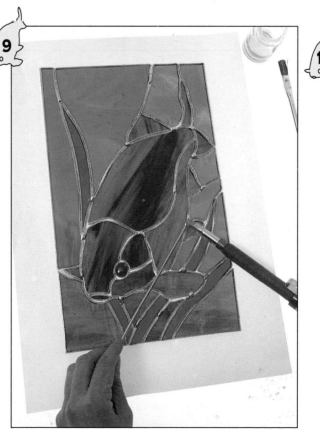

10 Apply flux along the seams and start to solder them. Touch the iron with solder while you move it along each seam, using enough solder to form a round "bead" along the seam. Turn over the panel and flux the back and edges. Lightly coat or "tin" on a thin layer of solder.

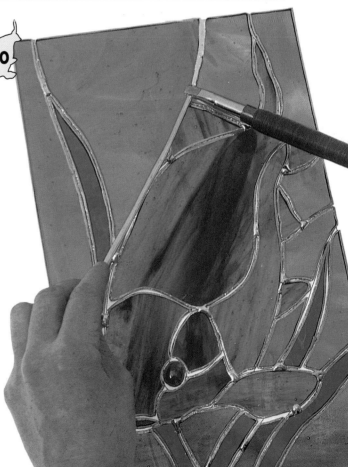

FURTHER INFORMATION

Cutting — pages 4–7
Filing — page 8
Foiling — page 8
Fluxing — page 8
Soldering — pages 8–9
Patina — page 10

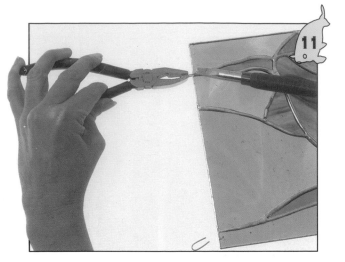

11 Solder wire loops into the seams.

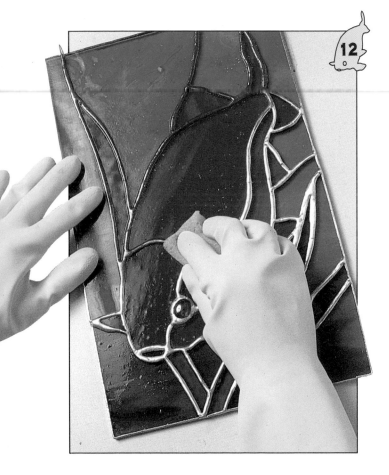

12 Wash thoroughly in warm, soapy water to remove any excess flux. Apply patina with a sponge, then wash thoroughly with warm soapy water.

LAMPSHADE

This shade will make an attractive side or table light when it is placed on a base. Use whatever colors of glass you like or ones that will suit your furnishings. Opal glass is not transparent, and you will need to make templates to place over the glass to trace around.

You will need
◊ 1 ¼ square feet amber-white opal
◊ ½ square foot pink-green opal
◊ 8 square inches dark purple cathedral
◊ ¼-inch copper foil
◊ 1 pound solder
◊ 1 x 2 ½-inch brass vase cap

Other equipment
◊ Scissors
◊ Felt-tip pen
◊ Straightedge
◊ Glass cutter
◊ Grozing pliers
◊ Glass file or carborundum stone
◊ Crimping tool
◊ Brush (for applying flux)
◊ Soldering iron
◊ Patina

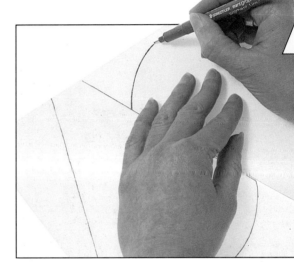

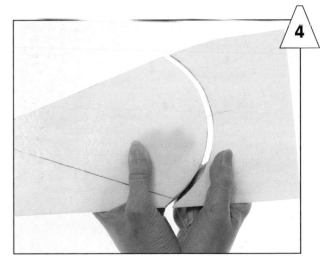

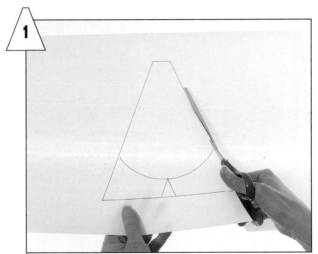

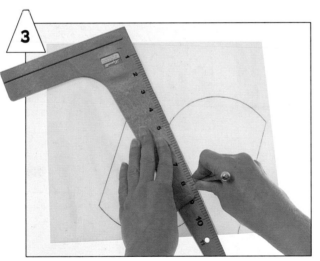

1 Enlarge and make three copies of the template. Cut out the pieces from one copy. Use a felt-tip pen to transfer the outlines to the glass.

2 You can cut the pieces most efficiently and economically by placing the templates side by side as shown.

3 Use the straightedge to position your cutter on the line and score by pulling the cutter toward you with a firm, even pressure. Score freehand along the curved section, pushing and pressing the cutter forward.

4 Tap underneath the curved score line until it begins to fracture. Only use your thumbs and index fingers to break off the curve if there is enough glass to allow you to get a secure grip. If there is only a small area of glass around the score line, use your pliers to remove it.

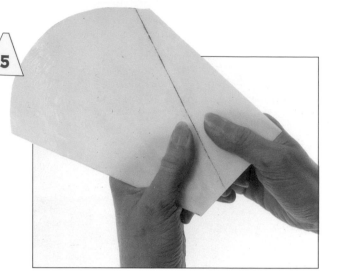

5 Use your fingers to snap off the straight edge. If the score does not seem to "want" to break, try tapping it on the underside to help fracture it.

6 Trace the pink-green section with the template and felt-tip pen. Use your straight-edge to score the line and break off the pieces with your pliers.

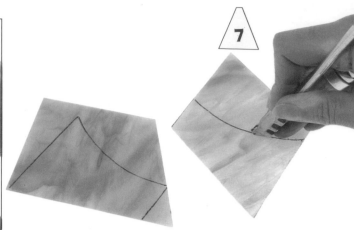

7 Follow the pen line to score the curve freehand with your cutter. Tap the underside and break off with your pliers. Cut out the small purple triangles.

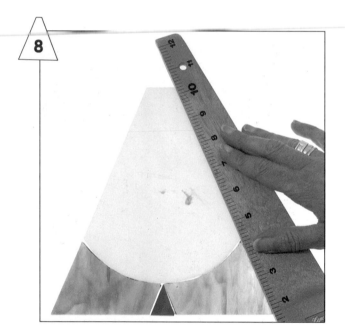

8 Check each panel to make sure that all the pieces fit neatly together and that the edges of each are straight.

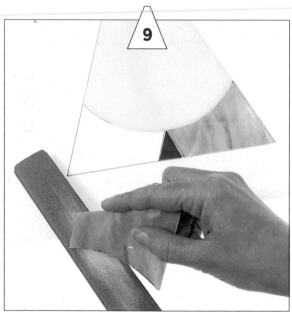

9 Smooth off any rough edges with a glass file and wash all the pieces.

10 Dry thoroughly and wrap copper foil around each piece. Make sure you center the foil accurately on the edge and overlap the ends by about ¼ inch. Use a crimping tool to smooth down the sides of the foil over the glass.

FURTHER INFORMATION

Cutting — pages 4—7
Filing — page 8
Foiling — page 8
Fluxing — page 8
Soldering — pages 8—9
Patina — page 10

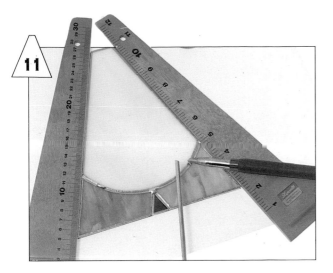

11 All the pieces in each panel now have to be positioned, fluxed, and tack-soldered, and you will probably find it helpful to use two straightedges to line them up.

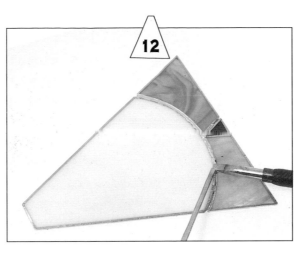

12 Solder along the seams, making an even "bead," then turn the panel over and apply a flat seam of solder. This will be the inside of the shade.

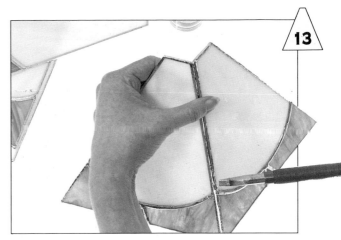

13 Begin to assemble the panels, tack-soldering along the top and bottom of the seams. As you tack-solder the panels together, the lampshade will take shape — there is no need to measure the angle between the panels.

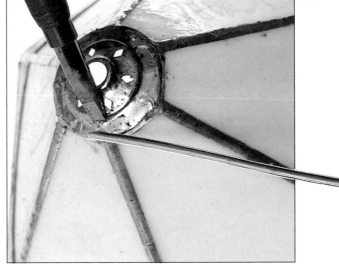

14 Assemble all the panels in this way until the last panel has been tack-soldered in position.

15 Soldering the vase cap in place will make the shape rigid. Center the cap on the top and solder all around the edge where the seams meet the cap. If you wish, tin the cap by fluxing the surface and very lightly soldering the brass surface. This will give the shade a more finished appearance.

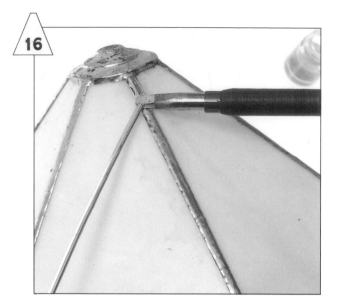

16 Flux and begin to solder the long seams. You will find it easier to achieve a smooth, even, beaded line if you are soldering along a horizontal plane, so prop the shade up while you work.

17 When you have worked around the outside, flux and tin on a thin layer of solder along all the inside seam. Use the smallest possible amount of solder, but make sure that you just cover all the exposed copper surfaces.

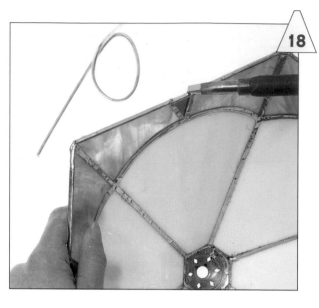

18 Flux and run a fine layer of solder along all the edges.

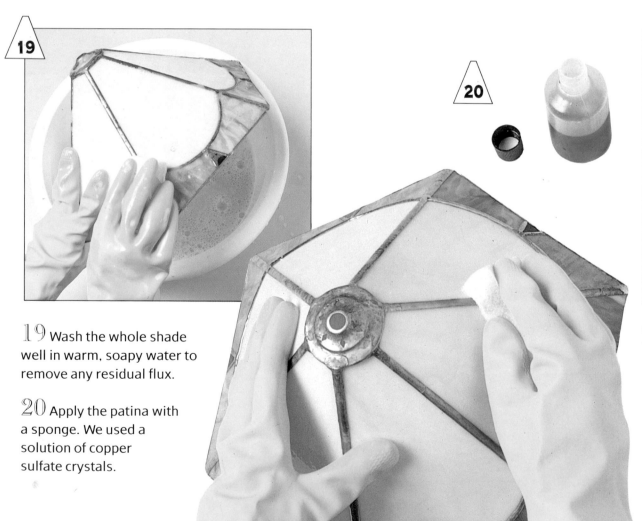

19 Wash the whole shade well in warm, soapy water to remove any residual flux.

20 Apply the patina with a sponge. We used a solution of copper sulfate crystals.

21 Wash thoroughly in warm soapy water.

CABINET DOOR PANELS

This project offers an opportunity to make a panel to fit an existing window or cabinet. You can adjust the size of the design as you wish. We have used it on a simple bathroom cabinet and have repeated the design on both doors, although the materials quoted here are adequate for a single panel.

You will need
◊ ½ square foot yellow cathedral
◊ ½ square foot light amber cathedral
◊ ½ square foot light blue cathedral
◊ ¼ square foot medium amber cathedral
◊ 8 square inches dark green cathedral
◊ 8 square inches dark amber cathedral
◊ ⁷/₃₂-inch copper foil
◊ 10½ ounces solder

Other equipment
◊ Scissors
◊ Felt-tip pen
◊ Straightedge
◊ Glass cutter
◊ Grozing pliers
◊ Glass file or carborundum stone
◊ Crimping tool
◊ Brush (for applying flux)
◊ Soldering iron
◊ Patina

FURTHER INFORMATION

Cutting – pages 4–7
Filing – page 8
Foiling – page 8
Fluxing – page 8
Soldering – pages 8–9
Patina – page 10

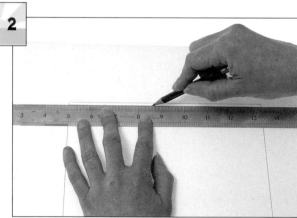

1 Measure the inside rabbet of the door-frame both horizontally and vertically.

2 Reduce the overall size by ¼ inch on each plane and draw the outline of the frame. Panels should always be made slightly smaller than the actual size of the rabbet so that you can fit the window easily.

3 Enlarge the template to fit the panel size. Use the grid method or photocopy it to the appropriate size. Alternatively, draw it freehand.

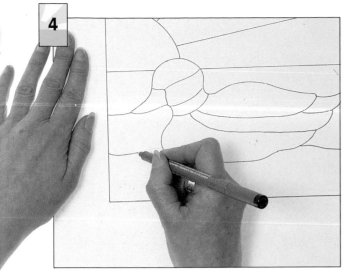

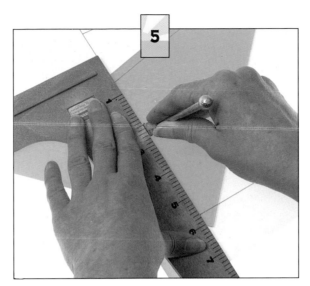

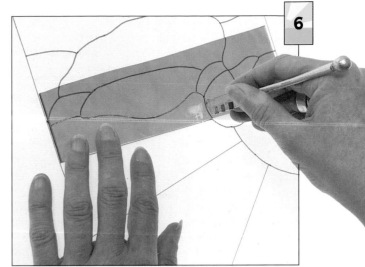

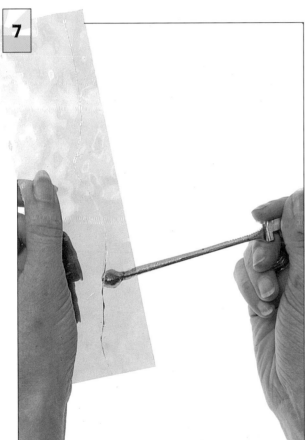

4 The lines extending from the central image of the duck are not only a design feature but are also technically important. The surrounding areas of glass need to be segmented to facilitate cutting.

5 When the drawing is ready for cutting, lay the appropriate colored glass in place. Use a straightedge as a guide when you score all the straight-sided pieces, pulling the cutter toward you.

6 Score curves by pressing and pushing the cutter away from you, following the pen lines.

7 Tap underneath the score line to fracture the glass, which should break apart easily.

8 Trim the edges with your grozing pliers.

9 Lay all the pieces on the template to check that they fit together well.

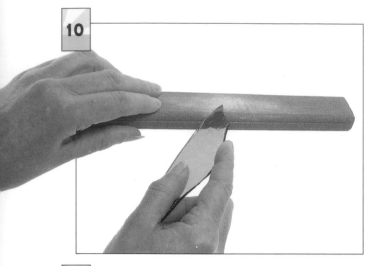

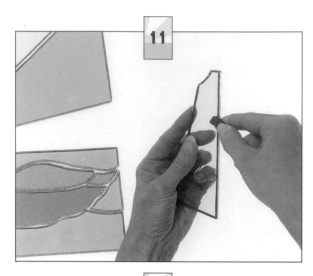

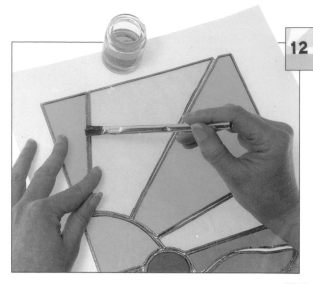

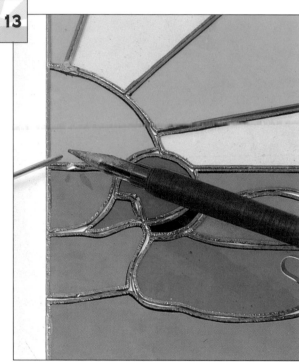

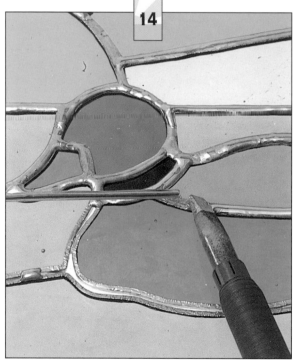

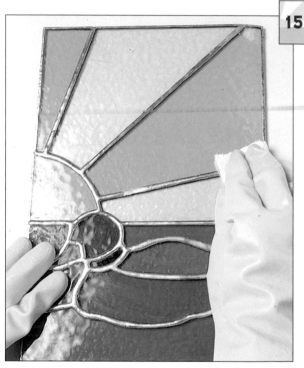

10 Remove any sharp protrusions with your grozing pliers and rub all edges smooth with a glass file or carborundum stone, then wash in warm water to remove all glass particles and smears of grease. Dry thoroughly.

11 Apply copper foil to all the edges, making sure that the tape is neatly centered on the edge and overlapping the ends by about ¼ inch. Crimp the foil smoothly onto the surface of the glass, squeezing it down to make sure that it is stuck along both sides.

12 Use a brush to dab flux at all the joints before you tack-solder the pieces together so that they do not move when you solder the seams.

13 Tack-solder all the seams, touching the tip of the iron on the copper to allow a small blob of solder to melt onto the spots of flux.

14 Flux all the seams and solder them, moving the soldering iron slowly and smoothly along the seams so that it forms a raised "bead." Turn over the panel, flux the seams, and apply only a small amount of solder to form a flat seam.

15 Wash the finished panel thoroughly to remove any residual flux, and apply patina with a sponge. Wash again thoroughly to remove the patina.

16 Place the completed panel in the door-frame with the flat-soldered surface toward you. Secure the panel in place with mitered wooden beading and brad nails.

TEMPLATES

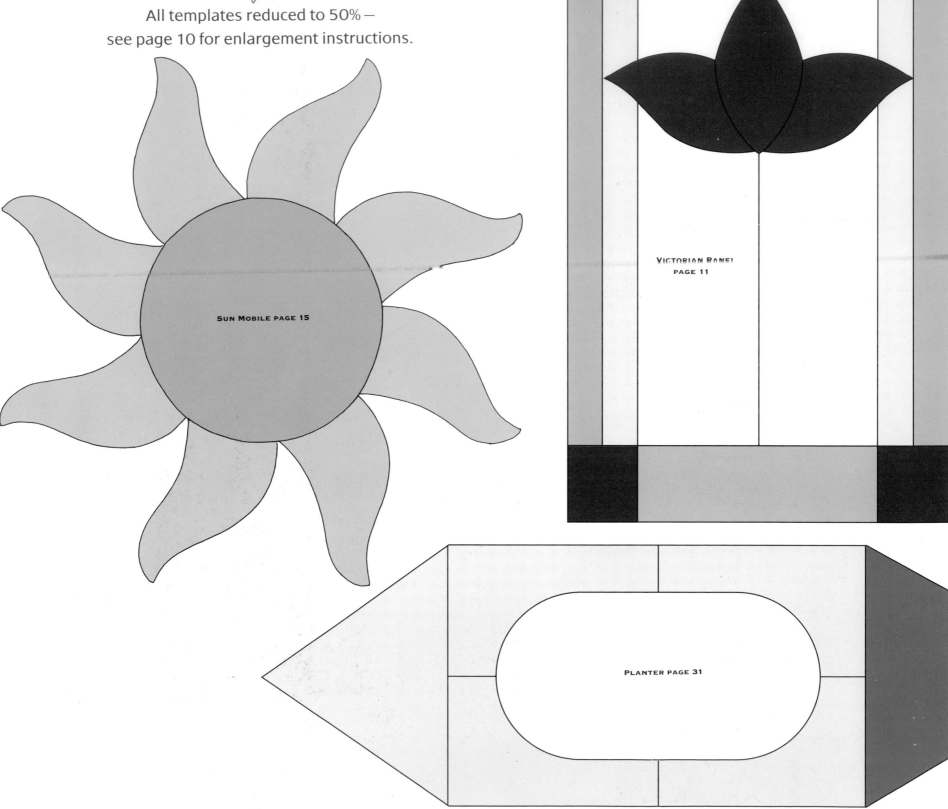

All templates reduced to 50% —
see page 10 for enlargement instructions.

Sun Mobile page 15

Victorian Panel
page 11

Planter page 31

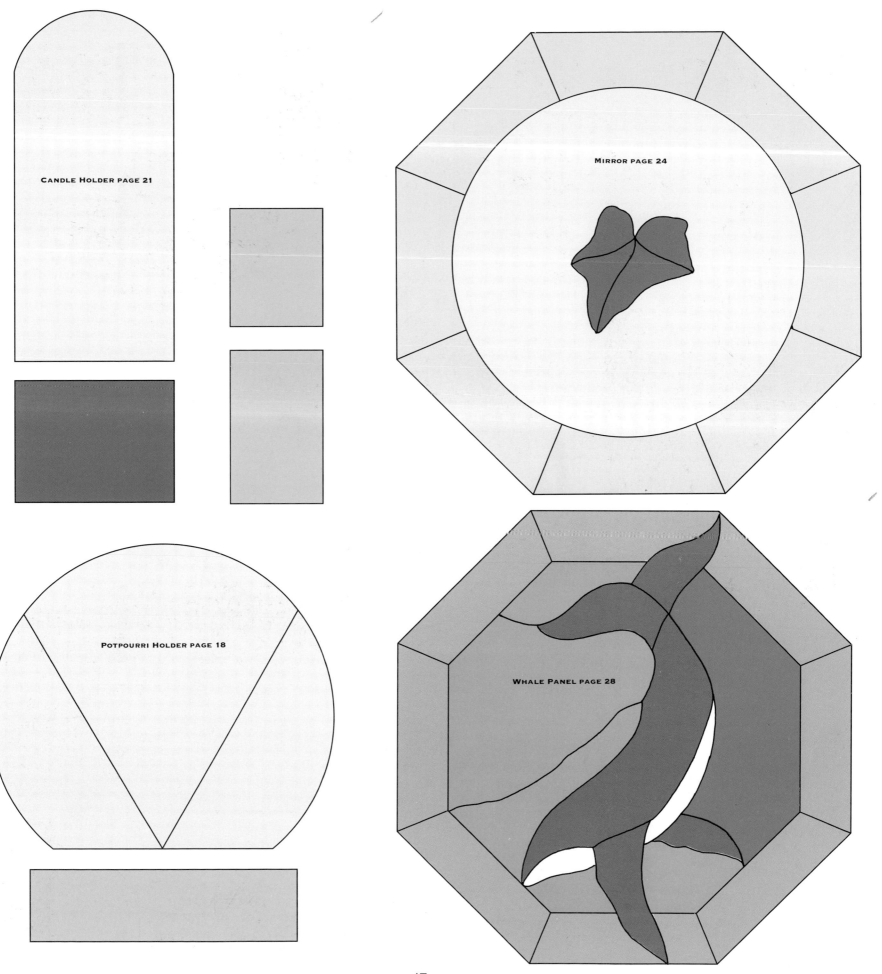

CANDLE HOLDER PAGE 21

MIRROR PAGE 24

POTPOURRI HOLDER PAGE 18

WHALE PANEL PAGE 28

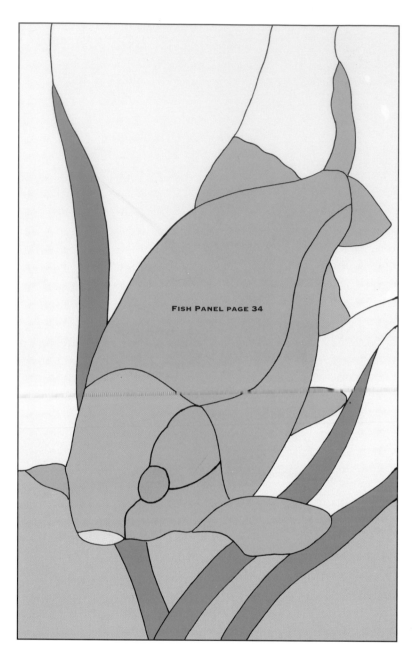

Fish Panel page 34

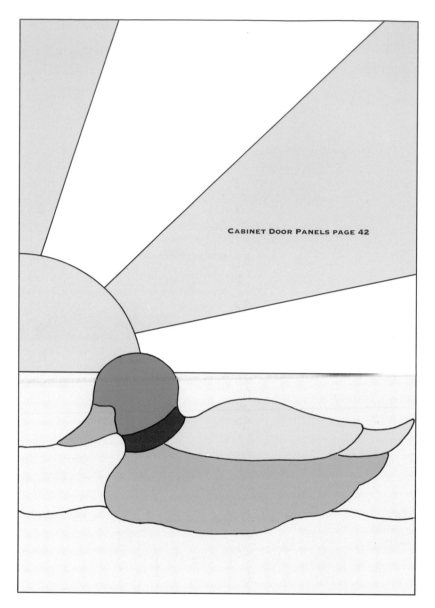

Cabinet Door Panels page 42

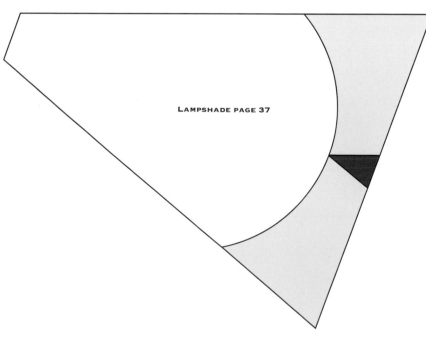

Lampshade page 37